A Word About
Gymnastics

By Lynne Gibbs   Illustrated by Shelagh McNicholas

ISBN 0-7696-3385-4

50395

9 780769 633855

School Specialty
Publishing

First published in Great Britain in 2005 by Brimax
Publishing Ltd, Appledram Barns, Chichester PO20 7EQ
Copyright © 2005 Brimax Publishing Ltd
This edition published in 2005 by Brighter Child®, an
imprint of School Specialty Publishing, a member of the
School Specialty Family. Printed in China.

Columbus, Ohio

Library of Congress Cataloging-in-Publication
Data is on file with the publisher.

Send all inquiries to:
School Specialty Publishing
8720 Orion Place
Columbus, OH 43240-2111

ISBN 0-7696-3385-4

2 3 4 5 6 7 8 9 10 BRI 10 09 08 07 06

The Warm-Up

If you take a class in gymnastics, you'll learn to flip, swing, somersault, and sail through the air!

Before you start, you will need to do what every athlete does—warm up and stretch. These gymnasts are performing gentle exercises to get their bodies ready for gymnastics.

What to Wear

Beginning gymnasts wear shorts or sweatpants and a t-shirt. For competitions, female gymnasts wear tight-fitting leotards. Male gymnasts wear singlets and tight sweatpants or tights.

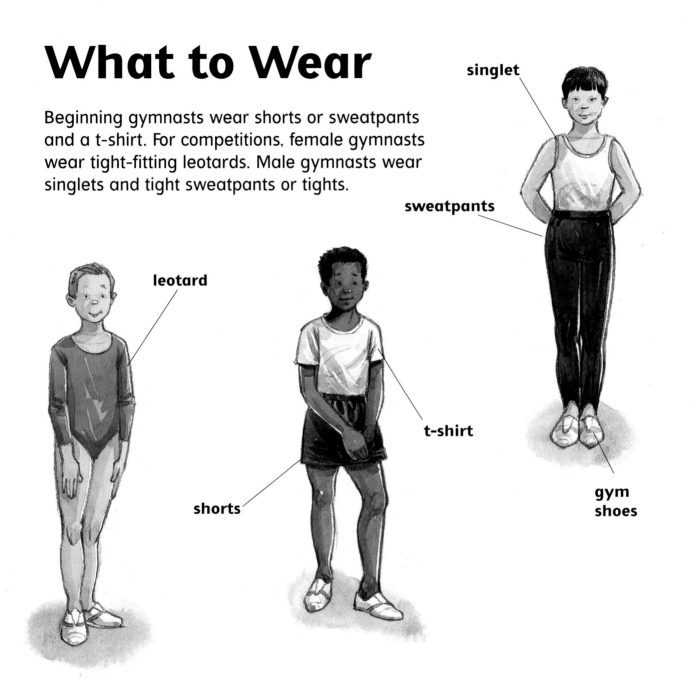

singlet

sweatpants

leotard

t-shirt

shorts

gym shoes

Warm-Up Exercises

Before starting any type of gymnastics, you need to do warm-up exercises. This makes your muscles more flexible and relaxed. It also makes you less likely to get injured.

To stretch your lower back and shoulders, grip a wall bar and press your head and chest towards the floor.

Stretching

After warm-up exercises, gymnasts stretch. These exercises help loosen, stretch, and relax different muscles in the body.

To stretch your thighs, kneel down on a mat and push your hips forward.

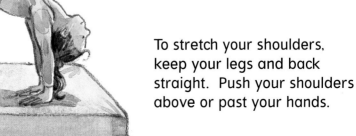

To stretch your shoulders, keep your legs and back straight. Push your shoulders above or past your hands.

Floor Exercises

Floor exercises combine dance moves and tumbling into a dramatic routine. The routine can feature jumps, leaps, and turns, as well as cartwheels, somersaults, and handsprings.

On the Floor

Both boys and girls participate in floor exercises. Girls perform their routines to music. Men's routines focus on power moves rather than dance. Their routines are performed without music.

the forward roll

1. The gymnast crouches down, keeping her back straight. Then, she stretches her arms forwards.

2. Leaning forward, the gymnast puts her hands at the sides of her head, keeping her head tucked.

the straddle splits

Gymnasts have to be flexible to perform this move. The back is held straight and the legs are stretched wide to form a straight line.

Floor exercises are performed on a special padded mat.

3. Pushing off with her feet, the gymnast rolls forward.

4. Then, she finishes in a squatting position.

the bridge

In this position, the gymnast arches her back with her stomach raised.

9

Rhythmic Gymnastics

Dance moves—plus special hand-held objects—are what sets rhythmic gymnastics apart. Gymnasts perform acrobatic dance routines using balls, ropes, hoops, clubs, and ribbons.

About Rhythmic Gymnastics

Rhythmic gymnasts dance to music, using dance steps and moves, while at the same time juggling with their hand-held apparatus.

ribbon

The gymnast makes spectacular patterns in motion as she throws and swirls a ribbon while she performs her routine.

hoop

Experienced gymnasts can swing or spin the hoop around their bodies. They can roll, throw, and catch it—and even pass through it.

rope

Although skipping is the main feature of rope work, gymnasts also swing the rope and throw it.

ball

The ball is carefully balanced by the performer as she gracefully bounces, rolls, swings, throws, and catches it.

clubs

One of the greatest tests of skill and balance is throwing and catching the clubs. Some routines also include swings and twirls.

Bars and Beam

On the beam, parallel bars, and uneven parallel bars, gymnasts perform routines made up of flying acrobatic moves and poses.

Girls perform routines on the beam and uneven parallel bars.
Boys perform on the parallel bars and horizontal bars.

Performing on the Bars and Beam

The balance beam and bar events require incredible strength and grace. The beam requires that a gymnast have strict body position and exceptional agility. The bars require extreme upper body strength and a sense of split-second timing.

balance beam

During a balance beam routine, the gymnast must move across the entire beam. The gymnast performs high moves and jumps as well as low moves, and moves from side to side. The dismount features a high jump or flip with a perfect landing.

uneven parallel bars

On the uneven bars, gymnasts perform swings, handstands, somersaults, and twists, swinging from a low bar to a high bar and back again.

horizontal bar

When gymnasts perform on the horizontal bar, they swing around the bar, change grip and body position, and perform release moves. During a release move, the gymnast releases and then grasps the bar again with the hands.

parallel bars

Gymnasts who perform on parallel bars display swinging and acrobatic moves on two bars placed side by side. The event requires strong arms and shoulders.

Vaulting

To be successful at vaulting, a gymnast must have speed, power, and courage.

A gymnast runs toward the vault quickly in long strides. Then, the gymnast jumps on a springboard and brings the hands to the vault. Next, the gymnast performs a series of acrobatic moves, such as round offs, handsprings, or jumps.

Vaulting the Horse

The vault, sometimes called the horse, is made of wood and steel. It is covered with padding and leather. A springboard sits in front of the vault to give the gymnast extra height. Beyond the vault is a landing area with a padded mat.

squat vault

The squat is a simple vaulting exercise for beginners.

4. The gymnast pushes off from the horse with the hands.

3. With the body in a vertical position, the gymnast places the hands on the horse.

2. The gymnast jumps up high from the springboard towards the horse.

1. The gymnast sprints toward the vault and hits the springboard.

5. Before landing, the body should begin to straighten with the arms stretched above the head.

8. Finally, the head and body must be straight, with the gymnast's arms by the sides.

6. As the gymnast prepares to land, the arms begin to come down.

7. On impact, the arms are lowered even more. The knees are bent and the feet should land flat on the mat.

Pommel Horse and Rings

Male gymnasts use the pommel horse and rings to perform routines in which they must support themselves with their upper body strength.

rings

This piece of apparatus requires greater strength than any other. Each routine must include swinging exercises with at least two handstands.

pommel horse

The gymnast's legs are not allowed to touch the pommel horse as he moves his body across and around the horse, making swinging, circular, and scissor movements. He must support himself on just his hands.

Competition

The largest gymnastics events are part of the Olympic Games and World Championships, where competitors from all over the world are judged for their gymnastics' skills.

Men compete in six events: the rings, pommel horse, parallel bars, horizontal bar, vault, and floor exercises. Women compete in four events: the vault and floor exercises as the men, as well as on the beam and uneven parallel bars.

Each exercise is given a score between zero and ten by a panel of judges. The scores are determined by how difficult the routines are and how well they are performed.

The overall champion is the gymnast with the highest total of points.

Glossary

apparatus Equipment, such as the balance beam or bars, used for different types of gymnastics exercises.

balance beam Apparatus used by females consisting of a narrow beam on which different moves and balances are performed.

bridge The gymnast arches the back while raising the stomach, resembling a bridge.

flexible Being able to bend the body easily.

floor exercises An event performed on a mat that may include acrobatic jumps, leaps, and turns, as well as cartwheels, somersaults, and handsprings.

forward roll A movement in which the gymnast crouches; leans forward, tucking the head; pushes off with the feet and rolls forward; and finishes in a squatting position.

parallel bars Apparatus consisting of two bars supported the same height above the ground.

pommel horse An apparatus used by gymnasts for vaulting. Used by males, the pommel horse has pommels, or handles, for gripping.

rhythmic gymnastics A type of gymnastics for females with a floor routine set to music, and hand apparatus, such as a ribbon, hoop, or clubs.

rings Apparatus for men consisting of gymnastics with swinging exercises, holding the body, and balancing events.

routine A set of moves that are joined together.

springboard Equipment used to give gymnasts extra height in vaulting or when mounting an apparatus.

squat A position where a person crouches with the knees bent and with the body weight on the feet.

uneven parallel bars Apparatus used by females consisting of parallel bars, one higher than the other.

vault An event that involves performing an acrobatic move, such as round offs, handsprings, or jumps over a vault, or horse.

warm-up Gentle exercises that prepare the body for exercise.